M000079634

The Seven Day Mental Diet

UPDATED FOR THE 21ST CENTURY BY
JACQUELINE GARWOOD

Sun Moon and Compass
149 Pine Street
Thunder Bay, Ontario
Canada P7A 5X4

Copyright © Jacqueline Garwood

Although this book is copyrighted material, the rules
that normally regulate such products do not apply
here. All thought belongs to the Universe and if what
you find in these pages helps you, please feel free to
share it with others. We are all linked together in a
Universal Network. The greatest compliment to this or
any work is in the sharing. May the words in these
pages touch as many lives as possible.

ISBN 978-0-9866808-3-0
First Edition April 2011

Also by Jacqueline Garwood:

Future Pull: Partner with the Universe to Create the Life of Your Dreams (Full-size Edition with Action Pages)

Future Pull: Partner with the Universe to Create the Life of Your Dreams (Condensed Edition)

Future Pull Life Creation Playbook and Journal

Dedicated to my sister, Ann.
Your calm and loving spirit inspires others.
If only they knew half the story ...

Contents

x

The Knots Prayer

Dear God:
Please untie the knots
That are in my mind,
My heart and my life.
Remove the have nots,
The can nots and the do nots
That I have in my mind.

Erase the will nots,
May nots,
Might nots that may find
A home in my heart.

Release me from the could nots,
Would nots and
Should nots that obstruct my life.

And most of all,
Dear God,
I ask that you remove from my mind,
My heart and my life, all of the 'am nots'
That I have allowed to hold me back,
Especially the thought
That I am not good enough.
Amen
~Author Known to God

Preface

The Seven Day Mental Diet, a small booklet read by many thousands of people since its creation in the mid-30s, is still fulfilling its promise—to change lives—eighty years later. Its author, Emmet Fox, remains one of the best known and most influential leaders of the New Thought movement.

Emmet Fox was born in Ireland on July 30, 1886. His father, a physician and member of parliament, died when he was just a young boy. Emmet graduated with a degree in electrical engineering, however, he soon discovered that he had a gift for healing and became interested in the metaphysical teachings of the New Thought movement.

New Thought encompassed a range of spiritual beliefs, from the Christian-based to pantheistic. Promoting personal freedom of belief rather than the dogmatic approach of most religions, New Thought took a practical, positive thinking approach to spirituality.

In 1914 the International New Thought Alliance was formed in London. Emmet, only twenty-eight at the time, joined the group and in 1928, he gave his first talk at Mortimer Hall. He must have felt he'd found his calling because, after moving to the U.S. a couple of years later, he became one of the most sought after speakers in New York. He became the minister for the Divine Science Church of the Healing Christ and gave lectures on New Thought to as many as 5,500 people, first at the New York Hippodrome and then at Carnegie Hall.

The message of the New Thought Movement, that each person has the potential to attract into their lives whatever they desire, must have been just what people needed to hear in the dark days of the Great Depression.

If that message sounds familiar, you're right. New Thought writers such as Emmet Fox, James Allen, Napoleon Hill, Wallace Wattles, and William Walker Atkinson are widely read and quoted now after being made famous by the 2006 book and film, *The Secret*. Far from being a secret, the Law of Attraction has been explained and promoted for centuries. However, it seems that William Walker Atkinson, writing under one of his many pseudonyms, was the first to call it the Law of Attraction in his 1906 book, *Thought Vibrations and the Law of Attraction*.

Besides becoming well known as a speaker, Emmet Fox was a prolific writer, producing numerous books and pamphlets, many of which are still in print today. One of his most famous is The Sermon on the Mount.

The Seven Day Mental Diet, although brief—it was only a few pages long—is one of Emmet's best known and most widely read works. The little book you now hold seeks to update the message for the 21st century while staying true to its underlying message—that you are what you think.

It's a testimony to the truth and power of its simple message that it can stand without any substantial change or correction so many years later. What was true in 1935—that what you think is what you attract into your life—is just as accurate today.

Initially, I intended this to be a minor updating of the language and references. In the end, however, it turned into a complete rewrite that includes seven principles to help you succeed in the Seven Day Mental Diet and real life stories and examples of how to incorporate the principles.

While conducting my research, I spoke to people who had attempted, and mostly failed, to keep the Seven Day Mental Diet for a full seven days. As Emmet Fox said, it may be simple but it certainly isn't easy. However, I did find a few people who not only succeeded but, as promised in the original title, changed their lives through the challenge. These generous and wise people shared what they had learned as they tried and tried again to finish successfully. Their hard-earned lessons are included here to make your journey easier.

I know, from speaking to people around the world, and from my own experience, that the

Seven Day Mental Diet will fulfill its promise. Just seven days and you will change your life.

Congratulations on taking this momentous step. When you have completed the challenge, I hope you will contact me at my website, www.JacquelineGarwood.com, and tell me your story.

Thank you.

"

Your own mind is a
sacred enclosure into
which nothing harmful
can enter except by your
permission.
~Ralph Waldo Emerson

"

Not Just Another Diet Book

In 1935, Emmet Fox began his Seven Day Mental Diet pamphlet with the following sentence, "The subject of diet is one of the foremost topics of the present day in public interest." Even then newspapers and magazines were filled with articles on diet and nutrition, and bookstores were filled with volumes unfolding the mysteries of proteins, carbohydrates, vitamins and minerals.

It is no different now, in fact, the interest in healthy eating has grown exponentially. A search of books on diet on the Amazon.com website brings up 53,073 titles. The last thing the world needs right now is another diet book.

No, this is not just another diet book. The Seven Day Mental Diet deals with the subject of dieting at a level that has even more profound and far-reaching effects than the food you eat. Physically, you become what you eat, but spiritually, emotionally and intellectually, you become what you think. Ultimately, your spiritual, emotional and intellectual health impacts your entire life. The Seven Day Mental Diet is the key to achieving success in every aspect of life from relationships to career and financial success and, yes, even your physical health.

Emmet Fox's Seven Day Mental Diet was a mere nineteen pages, small pages at that. In revising it and updating it for the 21st century, I'm going to follow his lead and keep it brief.

This book contains all of Emmet Fox's diet instructions, along with nuggets of wisdom gleaned from successful dieters from around the world. The resulting seven Guiding Principles will help you prepare for your life-changing week and stay on track for a full seven days.

One lesson I picked up when I interviewed people who had attempted, and often failed, to stick to the Seven Day Mental Diet for a full week, is that Emmet Fox was absolutely right when he said, "The Seven Day Mental Diet is not complicated but it is very difficult." Don't be discouraged by that statement. The eight Guiding Principles include the missing links that will mean the difference between failure and success.

The common thread that linked the successful dieters I spoke to was perseverance. They told me that they tried and, in the beginning, often fell prey to negative thinking by breakfast of the first day. Then they would try again, learning from their experience and adjusting and tweaking until they got it just right. Even then, they told me that a few weeks later, they would notice that they were falling back into bad habits. They would start over and retrain their brain again. Eventually, sometimes after many attempts, they realized that they had changed fundamentally and so had their lives.

Mark McManus is one such example. Mark is a Personal Trainer from Ireland and when I interviewed him early one morning, he told me that before the Seven Day Mental Diet, his default mood was negative. He was employed full-time and although he aspired to full-time self-employment, he never really thought he'd be able to support himself with his coaching business. Now, a full-time coach and personal development specialist, Mark says his default mood is positive. He contributed a great deal to this book, including Guiding Principles Two, Four and Six.

Shantel Springer, who was the source of much of the information in Guiding Principles Four and Seven, also tried the Seven Day Mental Diet over and over and over again. It wasn't until she understood the importance of becoming a conscious thinker that she 'got it'. Now, forty-five pounds lighter and a successful coach in Florida, Shantel is an international speaker and leads sold out 100 Days of Gratitude retreats. Shantel is an inspiring role model for anyone who has a dream and the will to accomplish it.

I spoke to Tim Brownson, a life coach and blogger from Florida, after reading his blog, A Daring Adventure. I was taken with his writing style; entertaining but down-to-earth. However, the main reason I contacted him was to discuss reframing as a tool to turn negative thoughts into positive. Much of Guiding Principle Five is based on my discussion with Tim.

The Seven Day Mental Diet won't be a walk in the park. Although if you enjoy the imagery of walking in a park, like another successful mental dieter, Terri Hartman, a publicist, producer and author from Florida, it might well be one of the tools that helps you succeed. Terri's suggestions are included in Guiding Principle Four.

This will definitely be the most challenging diet you've ever been on, but it's only for one week. Just one week out of your entire life and it has the potential to change your life in every way. After that week of complete mental awareness and discipline, everything will be utterly different and inconceivably better than if you had never taken up the challenge.

● ● ●

"

*Rules are not necessarily
sacred, principles are.*
~Franklin D. Roosevelt

"

The Rules

If you are at all like me, you have a house full of books, all of them well loved and thoroughly browsed, but few of them read completely from start to finish. I'm not alone, one source reports that 57% of new books are not read to completion; another claims that most people read only two chapters of a book before putting it aside. I believe the information in this book is so important that I want you to 'get it' even if you don't read past the first few pages. To this end, I'm making it ADD-proof.

I'll start off with the Seven Day Mental Diet in a nutshell. If you want, you can just read the condensed version and then take the plunge and start the Diet.

Then, when you reach noon of the first day and you've already let negative thoughts take root in your mind, you can come back and read the rest of the book—or at least scan it. It won't be a burden to review the seven Guiding Principles once, twice or even many times as you walk the hilly road to a consistently positive mindset.

Here are the rules of the Seven Day Mental Diet:

1. For a full seven days, you must not allow yourself to dwell on any negative thought.

2. Whenever a negative thought enters your mind, you must let it go.

3. If you do find that you have accepted a negative thought and allowed yourself to think about it for a period of time, even a minute, you have failed to keep yourself free of negative thoughts and you must stop the diet. After a period of time, start the seven days over again.

That's it! Three straightforward rules. Easy enough, right? Great! Begin...

●   ●   ●

"

All that we are is the result of what we have thought.

~Buddha

"

• • •

Guiding Principle One

You Are What You Think, And So Is Everything Else

This is the real key to a happy successful life: if you change your mind, you will change your life. When you change the way you think, your body and health, your relationships, your financial status, your environment, your daily activities, and even your feeling about your place in the Universe will change as a result. Everything in your life depends on your mental diet. The thoughts you think on a minute by minute basis, day to day, determine how your life evolves.

Let me give you a few examples. Your health is fundamentally affected by your thoughts. On a simple level, you make choices that affect your physical well-being. Many people make poor food choices based on their mood. If you eat to soothe yourself or eat when you're angry, frustrated or lonely, then your mind is controlling your health. If you are depressed and tired, you won't get the exercise you need to keep you in top physical shape.

We all know stress can kill. Although you may think stress is external—you are bored at work, not getting along with your partner, or your teenager is challenging your house rules—the reality is that stress is internal. Stress is your reaction to external events and your reaction is based on your perception and the way you think and feel about whatever is happening in your life.

Two people can be faced with the same situation—weather, debt, demanding boss, car problems, busy schedule—but have completely different responses. One person can take it on and brood or get angry or frustrated, while the other lets it slide off like they are made of Teflon.

One person ends up with the bad effects of the stress and the resulting health problems. The other doesn't.

Your home and environment is affected by your thoughts. If you believe that this is a Universe of scarcity, you may be inclined to hoard everything that comes into your life, resulting in clutter. Being surrounded by clutter makes day to day life more difficult, reinforcing negative thinking and adding to feelings of overwhelm. Feeling overwhelmed can lead to depression and cause you to procrastinate and put off taking action that can change your life for the better.

How about your career? As a career coach since 1981, I've seen the impact that negative thinking can have on client's careers and lives. I often work with people who are employed in toxic environments where they feel undervalued. They start to believe that they have no skills and few options, so they stay in a job that isn't satisfying or healthy for them. In reality, if they changed their thoughts about their job the results would be far different. First of all, their day to day experience on the job would change to reflect their new mindset. They would also have the confidence they need to take action and look for a different job.

The whole color and feel of your life will change as you change your thoughts. You will go from a depressed, angry individual to someone who can go with the flow, views obstacles as opportunities, looks forward to life and all it has to offer and is grateful for every minute of every day.

The Law of Attraction

Emmet Fox called it the Great Cosmic Law. Now in the 21st century it's commonly called The Law of Attraction and it's becoming the 'new normal'.   The Law of Attraction states that whatever things, people, events, opportunities and situations you think about, focus on and feel strongly about, you will attract into your life. This means that if you think about, focus on and feel strongly about things that you want in your life, they will show up, probably making you very satisfied with that Law of the Universe. On the other hand, it means that if you think about, focus on, and feel strongly about the things that you don't want in your life, they will also show up in your life. Not quite the outcome you'd like.

So you can see that it is extremely important to train your thoughts so that you think about, focus on and desire only those things that you want to attract into your life.

Your Thoughts Today Create Your Reality Tomorrow

The thoughts you harbored last year led to the life that you are living right now. Your thoughts last week have resulted in your present day reality. The thoughts you are thinking right now are going to determine the life you live tomorrow, next week, next month and next year. In fact, the present condition of every phase of your life was determined by the thoughts and feelings you fostered in the past, just as the condition of your life in the future will be entirely dependent on the thoughts you are choosing to entertain from this moment on.

In other words, you determine every aspect of your life as you choose your thoughts and allow them to take up residence in your mind. Thought is the real creative force in the Universe.

Change Begins on the Inside

You cannot change anything about your life—not in a lasting way—without changing the way you think. If you try to work from the outside in, changing your environment, your relationships, your health, or your activities, without working on your thoughts, you are doomed to failure.

The good news is that you can change your mind and, by extension, your feelings. They are totally under your control. You can become aware of your thoughts, monitor them, change them, and thereby change your entire life.

Who Rules? You Rule!

Because many of us move through life as though we're in a trance, believing that thoughts and feelings are beyond our control, we give up our power and responsibility for managing our thoughts and, ultimately, for living the life we desire. Many people don't understand or believe that we have complete control of our thoughts. In fact, our thoughts are all we can control.

The diagram below illustrates the different levels of power and influence that you have in your life.

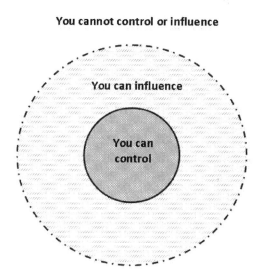

The inner circle contains those things that you can control; what you think, say and do. In the middle circle would be placed those things that you can influence. Notice that the line is broken, which is an indication that you can expand your influence as you learn to control your mind and fine-tune your skill at managing your thoughts and behaviors. Outside of the broken line are those things that you cannot control or influence. That would include things like the weather and the laws of the Universe, like gravity. What falls into each of the circles is largely determined by what you believe you can control or influence.

For example, in the innermost circle—what you can control—would be the thoughts you choose to harbor, the words you say, the messages that you choose to believe and to listen to. That circle would also include the food you eat, the material you read, the television shows you watch, and the activities with which you fill your time.

I'm always surprised at the response when I present this idea in workshops. Some people have joyful ah-hah moments, happy to recognize their power and excited by the opportunity to create massive change in their lives. Others will argue against it voraciously, refusing to accept that they have any power over their thoughts or even their behaviors. They say that 'they have no choice' as to how they perceive or respond to events in their lives. They say they do not control how they spend their time. They often give the example of taking a job that they don't want and, while they are at work, being required to spend their time at work as the boss decrees. And I reply, "Absolutely. However, you are not a slave and whether you choose to work or not, and work at that job or not, is your choice." Admittedly, the alternative may not be attractive, but you still make the choice.

Understanding that it is your choice is the first step in recognizing that you have the power to change everything—including the way you think about your job and what you focus on when you are at work. When you do not accept that you control your behavior, you give up your choices. In effect, you abdicate and give up your power and ability to live your life on your terms.

Power Equals Responsibility

So why wouldn't everyone be excited by the power they have to change their lives for the better? Because it means that they also have to take responsibility for their lives. If they believe they have no power or choice in how their lives unfold, then they do not have to take responsibility. They can blame it all on someone or something else. They can blame it on their parents and their dysfunctional childhood, on the economy, on the President, on the weather, or on the stars. Have you ever met someone who reads their horoscope every day so they'll know what to expect as their day unfolds? It's just another excuse for abdicating responsibility for their own behavior and, ultimately, for their own life.

We've already seen that what you think determines the quality of every aspect of your life. So it follows then that because you control your thoughts, you are in absolute control of how your life plays out. Because the Law of Attraction means that what you focus on consistently will come into your life, and because you have absolute control of what you focus on, you have ultimate power over what you attract into your life—the experiences, the people, and the opportunities.

With great power comes great responsibility. Once you accept that you have the ability to control your thoughts and change your life, you can no longer lay the blame on anyone or anything else. You can claim the power and the responsibility to create the life you want to live, or you can give up that right and abdicate your responsibility. Ultimately, that is also your choice. What will you choose?

●   ●   ●

"

It is only through
your conscious mind
that you can reach the
subconscious. Your
conscious mind is the
porter at the door, the
watchman at the gate.
~Robert Collier

"

· · ·

Guiding Principle Two

Wake Up! Become A Conscious Thinker

While the Great Cosmic Law or Law of Attraction is simple—you will attract into your life what you focus on—it isn't easy.

First of all, we aren't taught to be self-determining. In fact, it's just the opposite. We are told what to do, what to say, and what to think. We learn at a very young age to think and behave like everyone else in our family, social circle, country, or culture.

Our thoughts are so ingrained, and happen so automatically in response to any stimulus, that we don't recognize that we can actually choose them. But you can learn to step back and choose your thoughts. In fact, if you want to make your life happy and worthwhile, you must begin immediately, as soon as you realize you have that power and ability, to train yourself in the new habit of conscious thinking.

The Challenge

At first, you will find this extremely difficult. Depending on the source, it is estimated that the average person has anywhere from 1,500 to 15,000 thoughts a day. When I first read that, it led me on a convoluted path of contemplation and research. What exactly is a 'thought'? Do we have separate disparate 'thoughts' or a 'stream of thought'? With that many thoughts, how can we possibly screen them? We'd have no time to do anything else!

There are many ways to define 'thought', ranging from the philosophical to the biological and sociological.   Are thoughts really separate things—neurons firing in the prefrontal cortex perhaps? Or is thought an 'unbroken stream, moving forward without halt; past, present, future thoughts continuing as an unbroken stream'? Are thoughts like ripples in a pond—made up of waves of different lengths and frequencies? If they are waves in the energy of the Universe, what is the pebble that starts the ripple?

If thoughts are a continuous stream generated within our mind, can we possibly stop the flow, consider each one and then either accept or release it? Absolutely we can, but it requires that we step outside of our ego, our thinking self, and take the perspective of our greater self, the self that is part of the Universe.

Whether you realize it or not, you do this all the time. When you think about what you are thinking, you are stepping outside of your ego and viewing yourself and your thought processes through the eyes of your greater self. Try it now.

Right now, you are reading this page, decoding the print and the combinations of letters into words and processing the words into meaning. Now, in your mind, step back and 'see' yourself reading these words. Notice that you are now thinking multi-dimensionally. You are thinking on two levels; one is reading and processing the information on the page, while the other is recognizing and acknowledging that you are thinking about yourself as the 'reader'. You have stepped outside of your thoughts. You have connected with your greater self.

It's difficult to monitor every separate thought. It requires a great deal of focus. In fact, when you meditate, that's exactly what you're doing. You quiet the ripples in your mind and let it become still. The practice of meditation will help you become more adept at conscious thinking. I suggest you begin to adopt a daily practice of meditation. It will not only help you to become aware of your thoughts, it is restful and healing for both your mind and body.

But for now, let's get back to the challenge of conscious thinking on a day by day, minute by minute basis. Now that you have seen that you can think on different levels, you can begin to monitor the stream of thoughts that are flowing through your mind. It will require concentration and effort at first, but soon it will become second nature.

Start Fresh and Build Momentum

Mark McManus, who, after attempting the Seven Day Mental Diet many times, has been able to change his default mindset from negative to positive, suggests that you should start the Seven Day Mental Diet first thing in the morning. Choose which day to start, plan for it, and then, as soon as you wake up, immediately install a positive thought in your mind. Speaking from experience, he says that it is easier to maintain the habit of thinking positively if you get some momentum going rather than just deciding on a whim to change the way you habitually think.

As you move through your day, observe your thoughts. Most of them will be neutral and you can just let them flow through. Thoughts like, "I'd like a coffee", "Oh, its 8 o'clock", "What was that noise?"

Thoughts are auto-catalytic, which means that thoughts generate more thoughts. So a simple, neutral idea like, "I'd like a coffee" will lead to another thought such as, "Is it coffee time yet?" This will then lead to "Oh darn, it's only 9:00

o'clock.......Time seems to be dragging.......It's this boring meeting......I hate these stupid meetings..... What a waste of time." You can see how the thought stream started to head downward, into a mire of negativity.

When you become conscious of your thoughts, you can stop that trend and change the direction. So instead, you might think, "Oh darn, it's only 9:00 o'clock.....Time seems to be dragging.....It's this boring meeting"—STOP—"I will pay attention and see if I can come up with a good idea.....I'll enjoy the meeting more if I'm engaged."

It can also happen when you start to think about your possibilities, and negative thoughts can overpower your ability to attract what you desire into your life. It might sound like this, "I have an interview for that great job I want...that's great....but I am so bad at interviews...I'll probably mess it up and I won't get the job...besides there are probably lots more people who are better qualified...I don't know why I bothered."

Stop those thoughts immediately, instead, start thinking 'won't it be nice when...' thoughts. Then your thinking will go upward toward positivity rather than down into negativity. It will then sound like this, "I have an interview for that great job I want...that's great...but I am so bad – STOP – won't it be nice when I get the chance to tell them how I'm perfect for the job...won't it be nice when I am finished the interview and feel so great about how I did...won't it be nice when I get offered the job for more money than I make now and can start to think about buying a house."

At first it may feel stilted and false. The key is to stop the flow of thoughts when you become aware of thoughts that are not positive, helpful or constructive, and then make a conscious decision to either accept them or release them. When you notice that a negative thought has entered your stream of consciousness, ask yourself whether it is true and whether it is serving your greater good. You do not have to suddenly start talking to yourself in a phony, perky voice. You just have to consider whether a thought is of value to you and will help you as you create the life that you want to live.

If the thought is of value, keep it and move on to the next thought. If it isn't, turn it around or choose a different thought.

At first it will seem that it's all you can do to stop each thought at the door and make a decision—good thought, you can stay; negative thought, sorry no entry. Eventually, you will set up a sort of subconscious door. Most thoughts will just open the door and come in and you'll pay little attention because they are neutral or positive. Only the negative thoughts will set off alarms and cause you to stop them and make a decision.

Persevere

You will find conscious thinking rather exhausting at first. However, if you persevere it will become easier. Just as negative thoughts lead to more negative thoughts, positive thoughts lead to more positive thoughts. You won't have to work as hard to stop the flow of thoughts and you will begin to have a more robust supply of positive options from which to choose.

You will begin to bloom as you see how your life changes. You will have results almost from the moment you start the experiment and you'll be amazed at what you learn about yourself.

The Seven Day Mental Diet is designed to give you a good foundation on which to build. If you make up your mind to devote one week solely to building a new way of thinking, you will be able to carry it through even when distracted or faced with challenging situations.

If you devote one week to conscious thinking, it will become the turning point for you. It will be the most significant week of your life and you will be able to look back and say, "That is when my life changed."

"

One's philosophy is not best expressed in words; it is expressed in the choices one makes.
~Eleanor Roosevelt

"

* * *

Guiding Principle Three

Negative Thoughts May Knock But You Don't Have To Let Them In

The rules of the Seven Day Mental Diet, according to Emmet Fox, are very simple. "For seven days you must not allow yourself to dwell for a single moment on any kind of negative thought. You must watch yourself for a whole week as a cat watches a mouse. You must not under any pretense or for any reason, allow your mind to dwell on any thought that is not positive, optimistic, constructive, or kind."

Negative thoughts will come—no doubt about it—but you must immediately let them go. If you allow yourself to think the negative thought for more than a minute or two, you must stop the Seven Day Mental Diet and start it over again from the beginning. The reality is that negative thoughts will come to you; the trick is to let them flow in and immediately flow back out.

Emmet Fox said it's like sitting in front of a camp fire. If a hot ash flew out and fell on your sleeve, you'd end up with a hole in your jacket if you left it there to burn. But of course you wouldn't do that. Without thinking about it, you would immediately brush it off. That is the way you have to deal with negative thoughts—brush them off right away without allowing them to get a hold on your mind.

Recognizing a Negative Thought

You may be asking, "What exactly is a negative thought?" A negative thought is any thought of failure, disappointment, trouble, criticism, resentment, jealousy or judgment. So are thoughts of anxiety, helplessness, depression or fear. That includes any self-judgment, self-pity or self-criticism. Imagining or worrying about sickness or accidents or bad luck is also negative thinking. Any thought of limitation or pessimism is negative.

Any thought that isn't constructive, whether it's directed towards you or someone else, an animal, or even an inanimate object, is a negative thought. You don't need a list of negative thoughts to avoid. You will know when you have one, and when you know, you must reject it immediately. If your brain tries to deceive you and convince you that some random thought is neutral or 'realistic', your heart will tell you differently. Pay attention to your heart and body because it's less likely to trick you.

You can't pick and choose what you will allow or not. You can't decide that some negative thoughts don't count or don't matter. You can't decide, for example, that griping about the weather is okay but complaining about work isn't. The rule is that you can't dwell on a negative thought—any negative thought.

It's a Downpour of Negativity

You are constantly bombarded with negative thoughts and images. Television, radio and the internet sensationalize disasters, crime and heart breaking stories.

As I write this, cable news networks have been broadcasting non-stop images and stories related to a devastating 8.9 earthquake in Japan. That will continue until another crisis arises to take its place. I'm certainly not minimizing the tragedy in Japan. It was a terrible event and the death toll is climbing. Because the cooling systems in the nuclear reactor located in the region affected by the earthquake are damaged, the area is still under threat. Last year there was the oil spill in the Gulf of Mexico and the earthquake in Haiti. Living on this planet, in this Universe, with natural and man-made events of massive proportion happening on a fairly regular basis, there will never be a shortage of shocking, sad, and frightening news.

If you consider that each thought is a wave of energy, imagine the power unleashed by the thoughts of all the people in the world. With people around the world unified by thoughts of fear and sadness in response to events like the earthquake in Japan, imagine the power of their thoughts.

Do you really think that constantly focusing on the negative is going to help those who are affected? Wouldn't it be more helpful to send thoughts of love, healing and calmness? When you hear of terrible things, it does more good to release the negative thoughts and to replace them with thoughts of healing, love and calmness.

During the Seven Day Mental Diet, limit your exposure to negative news. Turn off the television and don't read the daily paper. Don't worry about being left out of the loop. If something is really important, someone will pass on the information.

Dealing with Negative People

Unless you are a hermit, you'll also interact with some people who have predominantly negative approaches to life. None of that matters. What matters is whether you pay attention to the negative messages that you hear from others and let them take up residence in your mind. If you are chatting with someone who is complaining and gossiping, don't bother to argue or take a stand. Remember the Law of Attraction. If you focus on what they are saying, get angry or try to resist it, you'll attract more of it into your awareness. Instead, just tune them out and change the subject.

If you are thinking, "Easier said than done," you are absolutely right. If you were never faced with having to turn your thoughts away from something unwanted, it would be easy. But that isn't an option in today's world. You'll have to resist negative thoughts and you'll have to triumph over them. That will build the strength of mind and forge the new neural pathways that will change your life forever.

Prepare for Challenges

What if you know that you are going to be faced with a challenging situation? If you haven't started the Seven Day Mental Diet yet, you may want to wait until the ordeal is over. On the other hand, remember that it is never the event or situation that is the problem. It is always your perception and your judgment of it that determines whether it is good, bad or neutral.

As you practice the Seven Day Mental Diet, you'll become much more skilled at monitoring your thoughts and identifying them as either positive or negative. You'll be able to receive all of the incoming messages, select those you want to recognize and accept and let the others flow on past you.

If you can keep it up for a full seven days, you'll find that at the end of the seventh day, you'll forget that you're on a diet and continue on with your new perspective and your new way of thinking. From that point forward, you'll find that your outlook and your life are changed forever.

●   ●   ●

Fill your mind with light, happiness, hope, feelings of security and strength, and soon your life will reflect these qualities.

.   ~Ramez Sasson

● ● ●

Guiding Principle Four

Do Is Stronger Than Don't

There are several 'mental laws' besides the Law of Attraction that, if followed, will help you during the Seven Day Mental Diet. One of these is the 'Law of Substitution'. Brian Tracy, in his book *Maximum Achievement*, explains the Law of Substitution this way:

> "It states that your conscious mind can hold only one thought at a time, and that you can substitute one thought for another. The 'crowding out' principle

allows you to deliberately replace a negative thought with a positive thought."

It's impossible to eradicate a thought from your mind unless you fill the space with something else. Try it for yourself. If I tell you not to think about a duck, what do you think of? Of course, you immediately think of a duck.

It's the same with negative thoughts. If you say to yourself, "I won't think about the snowstorm that we are having. I won't think about the snowstorm," I guarantee you will continue to think about the snowstorm. If, instead, you turn your thoughts to the warmth of your home, the glow of the fireplace, or the hot soup that you intend to have for supper, the thought of the snowstorm is forced out.

Let Positive Thoughts Push Out the Negative

Terri Hartman, a media consultant and publicist in Florida, also uses this technique. She focuses on inviting in the positive rather than pushing away the negative. This is how she makes the change from negative to positive thought,

> "What I do is so simple it's crazy. B.R.E.A.T.H.E. The key to breathing is to exhale first. Most people try to force air in where stress and distractions already fill the space. Instead, I blow it out gently, rotate my shoulders and then slowly inhale as I choose my thought, creating a movie in my mind. For me it's sometimes a park with sun coming through the trees. Sometimes I'm in the First Class Lounge of British Airways waiting for my flight to London. Nothing wrong with a good fantasy."

Prepare a Tool Box

How you respond to the inevitable negative thoughts will make the difference between whether you succeed on the Seven Day Mental Diet or not. It will help if you plan ahead and have tools ready to help you with this. For example, you can, like Terri, decide ahead of time what fantasy you want to focus on.

If you're stuck in traffic and start to have angry thoughts about other drivers, you won't be able to just 'stop' those thoughts. Be prepared to listen to motivational CDs on your commute to tune out any outside influences, while still keeping your mind on your driving, of course.

Mark McManus suggests that you prepare ahead of time with some tools to deal with challenging situations. For example, come up with a list of affirmations to install in your mind in place of negative thoughts.

Here are some turnaround phrases you can use to change your thinking, listed from the serious to the downright silly. Create some of your own, using your own slang and preferred imagery.

> "This thought isn't serving me. I will let this go and think about how beautiful my garden looks (fill in with a positive image of your choice). I should pick up some fertilizer on the way home."

"I can see that my thoughts are heading in a negative direction. Instead of thinking about what can go wrong, I am going to think about all the reasons why this is going to turn out great."

"It's too bad that happened but brooding (or sulking or getting mad – fill in your default negative response) isn't helping. I will think about ...."

"I am so lucky to be the one who decides what I focus on and how my life unfolds. Right now I choose to focus on and attract into my life only good things like..."

"I am the ruler of my mind and I decree that this thought is banished from my head. Bring in the dancers!"

"Bye bye negative thought. Welcome thoughts of joy, pleasure and abundance. Talking of abundance, I wonder if I won that $10 million dollar lottery last night."

"It is so cool that I can just change my mind in an instant. I love this power. I am WONDER WOMAN. Hmmm, that reminds me, I should have a costume party for Halloween."

Come up with a list of positive things that you can switch your attention to whenever you find a negative thought knocking at the door of your mind. They can include the people you love, people who make you happy, your pets, your accomplishments, or goals that inspire you. You can remember beautiful places that you've visited or think about upcoming vacations. You can make a list of uplifting books or music and keep them handy. Fill your mp3 or iPod with music that inspires you. Watch movies and television programs that make you laugh. Put a picture of a beautiful place, or a person you care about on your computer as a screensaver.

The options are limited only by your imagination. The important thing is to be ready so that when a negative thought enters your mind, you can use the Law of Substitution to replace it before it takes hold. At the end of the seven days it will have become a habit. You'll have seen the extraordinary changes for the better that occur as a result of eliminating negative thoughts. How could you go back when you have had a glimpse of the life that you can create for yourself with the power of your mind?

●　●　●

"

When you get into a
tight place and
everything goes against
you, till it seems as
though you could not
hold on a minute longer,
never give up then, for
that is just the place and
time that the tide will turn.
~Harriet Beecher Stowe

"

Guiding Principle Five

Re-Framing – How To Turn A Foe Into A Friend

When you do run into situations that are upsetting, disappointing or frustrating, you will be faced with the challenge of preventing negative thoughts from taking root, without trying to deceive yourself about the reality of the situation. For example, let's imagine that your car has broken down and you're faced with a big repair bill. No doubt about it, there's a strong likelihood negative thoughts will be knocking on the door.

You may be tempted to just give up and wallow for a while in anger, self-pity and a general bad mood.

How will that serve you? Does it help in any way to let a bad situation drag you down into depression or negativity? Will it help you solve the problem or deal with it in a more constructive manner? No, not at all. In fact, strong emotion like anger or depression can actually shut down your problem solving ability and can lead to bad decisions.

I'm not suggesting that you should lie to yourself and pretend that everything is great. You're not that stupid. I am suggesting that there are different perspectives from which you can view any situation and that you can step back and look at it from another viewpoint. That change of perspective is called reframing.

Try a Fresh Perspective

The key to succeeding at the Seven Day Mental Diet is to interrupt your thinking. Of course it's far easier to just carry on with your usual pattern of thought and, especially when you are dealing with 'trigger' situations—those that bring up the stronger emotions or memories—you have to make a conscious effort to STOP the stream of thought and turn it around. Reframing is one of the tools that can help you do so successfully.

Reframing is when you look for the good aspects of the situation, and believe it or not, there always are some. Sometimes they may not be obvious until you view it in hindsight but with practice you can learn to see them much earlier, even right away, in the middle of the difficult situation.

Tim Brownson, Florida Life Coach and co-author of *How to Be Rich and Happy*, talked about reframing in his blog, *A Daring Adventure*. He describes it as,

> "The act of taking a situation, event, interaction, etc. you feel negatively about and changing how you view, and thus, feel about it.
> If your favorite picture had a lovely frame round it that really made it pop, and I decided as a rather childish joke to

swap it with a hideously ugly one that made children weep, do you think it would change how you viewed the picture?

Of course it would, even though I haven't changed a thing about the content of the picture, I've changed the way you view it and there's nothing you can do about it."

He emphasizes that with reframing, you are never trying to change the content of the event; just the way you feel about it. He says that "Pretending to yourself an event was different to how it actually was just to feel better is delusional. It's also not very useful because you will start to distrust yourself." In his blog post on reframing, Tim gives an example: if he chipped a tooth while eating toast, rather than whining about the fact that he would have to visit the dentist and pay dearly for the privilege, he could reframe the situation by turning his thoughts around this way:

- It doesn't hurt;
- I wanted to make an appointment anyway for a check up;

- at least it wasn't a crown I broke."

On the same theme, I once broke off my front tooth just as I was embarking on a three-day kayaking trip off the coast of northern Vancouver Island. I had flown across the country, rented a car and driven up the length of the island to kayak with the whales and, just as we were packing the kayaks, I tried to open my poncho pouch with my teeth and snapped off my front tooth. The guide told me they weren't prepared 'to deal with pain' so I was forced to do some off-the-cuff reframing verbally so that they would let me go. I told them that:

- I thought it was probably a tooth I had a root canal on so I didn't really expect much pain;
- I had a bottle of scotch;
- I had a bottle of Advil;
- I had a high pain tolerance.

They let me go, and sure enough I had very little pain. However, I did look like something out of Deliverance.

Turnaround Phrases for Your Toolbox

Once again, it would be to your advantage to prepare ahead but coming up with some stock phrases to deal with negative situations. Here are some turnaround phrases you can apply when you are faced with a need to reframe:

"There is another way I can choose to see this. Let me see, what would be a good way for me to turn this around?"

"I can change the way I think about this and how it will turn out. In fact, this was a good thing because now I can …."

"This seems like a bad thing right now, but perhaps in the long term it might turn out to be a good thing. What are some of the ways this could play out that will be to my benefit?"

"What is the lesson in this for me? What can I learn from this to make sure I don't repeat this mistake?"

"

*Sometimes your joy is
the source of your smile,
but sometimes your
smile can be the source
of your joy.*
~Thich Nhat Hanh

Guiding Principle Six

Stand Up, Speed Up And Smile

Besides the Law of Substitution discussed in Guiding Principle Four, another 'mental law' is the Law of Reversibility. Neville Goddard, a contemporary of Emmet Fox, explained it this way,

> "If an effect (a) can be produced by a cause (b), then inversely, the effect (b) can be produced by the cause (a)."

For example, if magnetism can produce electricity, then electrical currents can create magnetism. Like most of the 'Laws of the Universe' taught by New Thought leaders, the Law of Reversibility is not only common sense but also backed up by scientific research. How will this help you stick to the Seven Day Mental Diet? It's very easy, probably the easiest and most fun of the Guiding Principles.

Positive Thoughts Leave Clues

If I told you there was a depressed person behind a screen and offered you $10,000 to describe him, would you be able to do it? Of course you could. You would probably guess that he'd be drooping, shoulders hunched, head down, face downcast.

You could just as easily describe a happy, excited, enthusiastic person. I'm sure you know from your own experience that when you are in a great mood you smile, stand straighter, walk faster and talk more quickly.

Many years ago, I recognized this in myself. I was self-employed and had just started a new training contract that would be very lucrative. The week before the training started I had applied for a loan to buy a new car and on the first day of the training I called the bank to arrange a time to go and sign the papers.

The training was held in an abandoned wing of an old tuberculosis sanitarium—very eerie, actually. During the first break of the day, I bounced down the hall to the phone to call the bank. I literally felt like I was walking on air. Great new project with fun people, a new car all picked out and ready to be purchased—everything felt like it was going my way.

When I talked to the loan officer, she told me that it had been turned down because I was self-employed. They just didn't feel like I was as a stable as someone who had a regular job. The loan officer offered to resubmit my application if I could show her I had a predictable income. I promised to get back to her but all my happiness had escaped as if it was let out of a balloon.

I trudged back down the hall to my next session, feeling like suddenly there was a lot more gravity holding me down. I felt like I could barely lift my feet.

At noon I went and gathered up the required paperwork and took it in to the bank. Later that afternoon, I called again and found out I had been accepted. All of a sudden, it felt like there was less gravity and I was standing straighter, walking more quickly and speaking in a lighter, faster voice.

Now, whenever I have a day where I am feeling down for some reason, I refer to it as a heavy gravity day. Light gravity days are those where I am happier and lighter.

The Law of Reversibility means that if you know how you hold your body and face and how you behave when you are happy and positive, you can then create that feeling by 'acting as if' you are happy regardless of your actual mood. If you speed up your rate of speech and your movements, smile, raise your eyebrows, open your eyes, look upward, stand straighter, you will start to actually feel happier and more positive. Like the Law of Attraction, it's a powerful law of the Universe that you can use to your advantage.

Act As If

There's plenty of evidence that 'acting as if' can be very effective in changing emotional states. In a study at Wake Forest University in North Carolina, a group of fifty students were asked to act like extroverts for fifteen minutes in a group discussion, even if they didn't feel like an extrovert. They found that the more assertive and energetic the students acted, the happier they became.

'Acting as if' is often used as a therapy technique for dealing with depression. Patients are instructed to go through the routines of life as though they are enjoying them even though in reality they are depressed. Initially, it may feel forced or fake, but eventually their mood starts to reflect their behaviour.

Kathy Delaney-Smith is a shining example of how to 'act as if'. In 1998, Kathy, as Head Coach, led the sixteenth-seeded Harvard Women's Basketball team to victory over top-ranked Stanford in the N.C.A.A. championships. Stanford had one of the strongest women's programs, had won the national title twice and had a 59-game home winning streak dating back to the 1993-94 season.   Harvard, on the other hand, was considered to be heavy on brains but light on athletic potential. But Harvard had Kathy and her 'act as if' philosophy.

Kathy Delany-Smith would tell her team, "Act as if you're not tired. Act as if you're confident. Act as if you're the best player because if you can do that, then you can get really and truly closer to it." She did not allow players to show weakness even during practices. Yawning wasn't allowed. If they fell they had to get up within three seconds. She said, "We're all too busy verbalizing and saying what's wrong when we could be stronger and better if we envision what's right."

When you 'act as if' you apply the Law of Reversibility as well as the Law of Attraction. 'Acting as if' you are positive, upbeat and enthusiastic will lead to real changes in your mental state. If you 'act as if' you are having a great day, any negative thoughts will be pushed out and replaced with positive thoughts. Those positive thoughts will actually result in positive things being attracted into your life. You will find your day turning around and it will no longer be an effort to think more positive thoughts.

In other words, if you smile even when you have nothing to smile about, you'll find that soon you will have something to smile about.

•   •   •

"

We tend to forget that happiness doesn't come as a result of getting something we don't have, but rather of recognizing and appreciating what we do have

~Frederick Keonig

"

● ● ●

Guiding Principle Seven

Appreciate The Positive And The Positive Will Appreciate

Although this Guiding Principle is last it really is important enough to be first. It is integral to all of the other Guiding Principles. As you learned in Guiding Principle One, what you think about is what you attract into your life. When you focus on the good things in your life, the good things in your life will continue to be part of your life and, in fact, will grow and become more abundant.

Appreciation or gratitude can turn your thoughts around in an instant. If you are going through a rough patch, stop for a minute and think of all the good things in your life. You will find that your attitude and mental and physical strength is increased and you'll feel like you can easily cope with anything you encounter.

Count Your Blessings

When we count our blessings, invariably we will have more to count. I remember when I first started to keep a gratitude journal and how just the act of listing my blessings turned me around from misery to joy.

It was in 1996 and I came home from work all tuckered out. As soon as I walked through the door, I saw that chaos had visited my home while I was gone. Ruby, my German Shepherd, had carefully carried a pot full of borsht from the kitchen sink to the middle of the living room and spread it around while she had a leisurely lunch. I guess the beet soup didn't agree with her because then she vomited all over the carpet as well.

It appeared that she then tried to hide the mess by dragging my beloved peace lily over and spreading it around over the mess. I got some towels and started scrubbing. I did the best I could with just towels and a bucket of water, figuring I'd have to rent a carpet cleaning machine as soon as possible.

Then I went to put the now purple towels into the washing machine and found that the laundry I had put in there in the morning was sitting in a machine full of water. My washing machine had broken down. So I pulled everything out of the tub and put the soaking wet clothes into a laundry basket with the purple towels. As I carried them through the living room to the front door I realized that all the water was dripping all over me and down onto the floor. I was leaving a trail of dirty water all through the house.

So I had a little cry and then went to the Laundromat to wash and dry everything. I was feeling very low. It was one of those days where you just want to lay in bed, drink a bottle of wine and listen to country music. As I sat in the Laundromat waiting for my clothes to dry, I took out a small piece of paper and started listing all the bad things that had happened that day. Like I needed verification or something. When I finished my list, I looked at the list and counted ten things. Ten nasty evil events. It was definitely a heavy gravity day.

Then I had the idea to write down a list of all the good things that had happened that day. When I finished I was dumbstruck. There were thirteen good things. The good outnumbered the bad. I was able to find good things to appreciate and be grateful for even on that terrible day. My mood was changed in an instant. It was suddenly a light gravity day and I was full of energy again.

Make Gratitude a Habit

Since that day in the Laundromat, I have made it a habit to end my day by writing a list of all the things in my life that I appreciate. Not only do I do that on a daily basis, I do it whenever I feel that I am starting to feel hard done by and when I'm starting to focus on the negative rather than the positive.

Coach Shantel Springer leads one day retreats where she launches people into 100 days of gratitude. You can start with just seven days. During each day of the Seven Day Mental Diet, stop several times and turn your attention to everything that you appreciate in your life.

Here's a suggestion so you won't forget: set your watch or cell phone to alert you three times during the day. At that time, take out a piece of paper and list all the good things in your life. Don't just think about them. Write them down. It will make it so much easier to maintain the challenge of the Seven Day Mental Diet.

There! Those are the seven guiding principles that will help you to successfully finish the Seven Day Mental Diet. Each one of them is a powerful tool that can help you eliminate negative thinking from your life and turn your life around in only seven days.

● ● ●

"

And when things start to happen, don't worry. Don't stew. Just go right along. You'll start happening, too.
                    ~Dr. Seuss

"

What You Can Expect

You will probably start off the Seven Day Mental Diet full of optimism and confidence. Most people find that within one day they are challenged and some even give up before the day is over. In fact, all of the people I talked to who were successful Dieters told me that on the first day they quit before lunch time. So don't feel like a failure if it happens to you. Just follow their lead and try, try again.

You may find that something else happens when you embark on the Seven Day Mental Diet; something odd. You may find that starting the Diet seems to stir up all sorts of difficulties. Everything begins to go wrong at once. Even physical issues rise up—headaches, nausea.   Perhaps it's your body's way of maintaining the status quo.

These are challenges to the whole intent of the Seven Day Mental Diet—the point is to completely refuse to let any negative thoughts take hold in your mind.   And what happens? Difficulties arise that cause you to start thinking negatively. Is it a conspiracy? No, of course not, and that's just negative thinking.

When your whole world, physically, emotionally and spiritually, starts to rock, just hold on and let it rock.   It means that things are moving. Your world is changing. That's what you want. When the rocking is over, the world as you know it will have reshaped itself into something that is much closer to the world you are meant to inhabit.

When the Seven Day Mental Diet is over, you will be a different person. You will have a completely new outlook on the world, a new way of looking at things. You will make a conscious decision to choose your responses to events rather than just reacting mindlessly. You won't be at the mercy of your thoughts and moods. You will be steering your own boat, not just clinging desperately to the life raft that keeps you afloat in your life. You will be a self-determining person who chooses your life course and then takes action to achieve your dreams.

This isn't the end of the Diet. It's the beginning of your life.

●   ●   ●

Never doubt that a small group of thoughtful, committed citizens can change the world. Indeed, it is the only thing that ever has.

~Margaret Mead

Now That You Have Changed Your Life, Change The World…

Congratulations! You did it. You took the challenge to think nothing but positive thoughts for a full seven days. I'm sure that you have changed as a person and that your life has changed as the result of your efforts to turn your thinking around. Now are you ready to take on an even greater challenge?

You know that your thoughts can change your life. You've seen that principle in action and experienced its power. But just imagine….if you can change just one life, your own, with the power of thought, what can the energy of many thoughts do? Imagine the power of a positive thought multiplied by the billions of people now living on the earth. What could we accomplish if we all united in powerful positive thought?

Imagine a world where everyone has enough to eat. Imagine a world where everyone lives in peace. Imagine a world where everyone feels loved and valued. If we can imagine it, we can create it.

Now that you have experienced the power of thought, pass it on. Help to spread the word that we have this amazing power and that we can create a world of peace, love, abundance and joy. Every thought will make a difference. Every voice will make a difference. You will make the difference. Never forget your power to change the world.

"

*Consider the postage stamp:
its usefulness consists in the
ability to stick to one thing
till it gets there.*
~Josh Billings

"

Acknowledgements

I must acknowledge the work of Emmet Fox. It was from his pamphlet, The Seven Day Mental Diet, that this book grew. His works are widely available on the Internet and continue to inspire people worldwide.

Neville Goddard's writing on the Law of Reversibility, Thinking Fourth Dimensionally, and the Law of Substitution allowed me to explore other approaches to creating a positive mindset.

I would also like to thank the following contributors for their wisdom, insight and inspiring stories:

Mark McManus, a Personal Trainer from Ireland, owns the popular bodybuilding and fat loss site, MuscleHack.com. He has also written for top bodybuilding publications and is the author of the book, *Total Six Pack Abs* and the creator of the bodybuilding system, *Targeted Hypertrophy Training*. His latest project is HappyHack.com, a website focused on how to be happy, successful, and achieve peace of mind.

Terri Hartman, a Publicist, Producer and Writer from Florida. After twenty-five years representing clients, including Bob Hope, Forrest Whittaker and David Hasselhoff, in Los Angeles, Terri now works from her patio garden in Florida. Her client list now includes Universal Studios Florida Production Group, George Foreman, and author Fannie Flagg.

Shantel Springer, mother, wife, self-development coach, and international speaker. A woman who changed her life by unlearning toxic thinking, and patterns, Shantel formed a 'Healthy Mind' and created a 'Healthy Body'. When she let go of limited beliefs and started living her life from a state of Gratitude, she lost 45 pounds and transformed her life. She is a renowned expert in

M.B.S. 'Mastering Belief Systems'. Her book, *Master your Belief System and your Finances*, will be released 2012. You can contact Coach Shantel at www.100daysofgratitude.com.

Tim Brownson, an author, certified Life Coach and NLP Master Practitioner. Tim runs the *A Daring Adventure* blog (www.adaringadventure.com), one of the most popular self development blogs in the US. He is also involved in a project to give away to good causes 1,000,000 copies of a book he co-authored called *How To Be Rich and Happy.*

Resources

You are invited to visiit www.FuturePull.com or www.JacquelineGarwood.com to download the e-book version of the Seven Day Mental Diet Journal.

At the website, you'll also be able to sign up for the newsletter and find out about upcoming MasterMind groups, teleclasses and group or one-on-one coaching. These programs and resources will provide inspiration and support and as you create the life of your dreams.

About the Author

Jacqueline Garwood is a catalyst, coach and celebrant, helping clients to see the unlimited possibilities, find their adventurous spirit and walk their unique life path with joy and gratitude. She has been leading Law of Attraction workshops and retreats since 1989. She is the author of *Future Pull: Partner with the Universe to Create the Life of Your Dreams* and the *Future Pull Playbook and Journal*.

Jacqueline lives in Thunder Bay, Ontario, Canada with her dog, Charlie, and cat, Kitty. Whenever possible, she travels to Ottawa to visit her son and his family. She is available for workshops, retreats and presentations.